In a time when many in our society struggle loneliness and isolation, the Biblical calling to please God by showing hospitality is especially needed. This concise and thoughtful guide will challenge you to grow in your effectiveness at loving your neighbors through invitations to dine at your table. With relatable life experience examples, authentic prayers, and insightful questions, retired Pastor Timm Oyer's book equips readers to serve others through meaningful and intentional hospitality. So, spend some time with these thoughts from Pastor Timm and serve salt and light at your table.

-Heather Cartwright, Attorney
Retired U.S. Department of Justice

We have all heard the story of the Last Supper where Jesus called his disciples together to share His last meal. What you may have missed are the many other times Jesus used the table as part of His ministry. Pastor Timm's new book, "Dinner with Jesus" explores the ways in which Jesus used shared meals to spread His message of love, friendship, inclusion, and obedience to God to both believers and non-believers. He also recalls the impact of some of his own meals with family, friends, and strangers, and suggests ways in which we may all transform our own shared meals into sanctified experiences. Thought-provoking prayers and insightful short questions at the end of each chapter offer more opportunity for reflection and discussion. This book will provide a starting point for you to evaluate your own approach to sharing meals with others.

-Guy Wood, Traverse City, Mi
Collector/Curator, Peninsula Books

What happens around the table? Family tables, sacred tables, sharing a meal, breaking bread. Written with warmth from his own personal experience, Pastor Timm Oyer invites us to the table of Jesus. His insights from scripture as well as the stories of family will warm your heart and perhaps touch your soul. The book invites conversation about what happens around out tables and what can happen around the table of Christ.

-Rev. Dr, Jack Harnish [Retired]
United Methodist Church

Then Jesus declared, "I am the bread of life. Whoever comes to me will never go hungry, and whoever believes in me will never be thirsty."
John 6:35

Here I am! I stand at the door and knock. If anyone hears my voice and opens the door, I will come in and eat with that person, and they with me.
Revelation 3:20

Every day they continued to meet in the temple courts. They broke bread in their homes and ate together with glad and sincere hearts, praising God and enjoying the favor of all the people. And the Lord added to their number daily those who were being saved.
Acts 2:46-47

So, whether you eat or drink or whatever you do, do it all for the glory of God.

Corinthians 10:31

To Sherry, my wife, my love, my best friend.

Timm

Prologue to Dinner with Jesus

Exploring table ministry and the table talk of Jesus, images of my family dinners flash across my mind. Dinner at my house was always an important occasion in our daily lives. Dad would always open with a prayer of thanksgiving beseeching God's blessing on the meal we were about to share. His prayers were always short and focused though I don't remember any exact wording, they were never trite, always fresh. When asked what I remember most about growing up, it is our family meals. Except for a rare, excused absence, every member of our family was expected at the table for dinner. Regardless of our daily events there was always the anticipation of Mom's home cooked meal and lively conversation. Trivial matters were suddenly relevant and silence rarely golden. No topic was off limits for discussion as long as civility reigned.

One of my favorite table memories is when our family was invited to share a meal with the parents of a teen who attended our youth group at the first church I pastored in Kutztown, Pennsylvania. The teen told us his parents rarely attended church, so there were no expectations as we sat at the table. His father invited us to sing a

Psalm. Regretfully I don't remember the specific Psalm, but it was a beautiful praise for the meal and a personal Emmaus Road experience I will never forget. His father pleasantly surprised us by singing scripture!

My wife Sherry has fond memories of regularly going to her grandparents' house on Sundays for family dinner with aunts, uncles and cousins. After marrying Sherry, I was fortunate to attend one of those gatherings. To this day her family continues to share family favorites at their annual reunion. These gatherings are times of bonding and encouragement for everyone present.

NPR'S Nina Totenberg says in her new book Dinner with Ruth "One trade secret that I have found for making and keeping and nurturing friendship is the act of sitting down together for a meal".[1]

In Matthew 11:18-19 we take note that the Pharisees did not understand Jesus' emphasis on table fellowship. Table talk with Jesus was important, but the naysayers were not of the same opinion. To Jesus, table talk was more than an act of hospitality or kindness; it was an intentional act of spiritual discipline. His main goal was to present the Gospel and to be inclusive with everyone.

"For John the Baptist didn't drink wine and often fasted, and you say, 'He has a demon.' The Son of Man eating and drinking, and they say, 'Behold a gluttonous man and a drunkard, a friend of tax-collectors and sinners!' Yet wisdom is vindicated by her deeds." -Matthew 11:18-19

Jesus shared table talk with Matthew and his tax collecting friends. He invited Himself to Zacchaeus's dinner table to personally share the good news. Both examples prove the Pharisees correct in their accusation that Jesus wanted to be a friend to tax collectors and to sinners and always will be.

At times the disciples were tragically slow to grasp the meaning of table talk with Jesus', and we often are as guilty. We attempt to cover our lack of understanding under the umbrella of hospitality, increasing the danger of diminishing the connection between our table and God!

I can think of no other person, in scripture or my life, whose full character is on such display at the table as Jesus. I confess at times my table prayers are little more than thanks and seeking God's blessing on the food about to be eaten.

It's been written table fellowship is one of God's love languages. Every time we read scripture of Jesus dining experience, our hearts are suddenly warmed and challenged. Today we wouldn't think of inviting ourselves to someone else's table or at times inviting the "least of these" to our table as Jesus did. Our social etiquette tends to stop any spiritual impulse to do so, but we're so glad Jesus set the example for us.

In Luke's gospel, Jesus gives us guidance in preparing our meal talk.

***Luke 14:12-14** "When you give a luncheon or dinner, do not invite your friends or your brothers or your relatives or your rich neighbors, lest they also invite you in return, and repayment come to you.*

But when you give a reception, invite the poor, the crippled, the lame, the blind, and you be blessed, since they do not have the means to repay you; for you will be repaid at the resurrection of the righteous.

I don't believe this admonition is intended to leave out those whom we enjoy eating with, but to not make them our only invited guests.

Except for a standing invitation at Lazarus' home, we don't hear of anyone inviting Jesus back to their table a second time. This can trigger many questions and may become a reason there are people we never invite back because we have become uncomfortable with their straight forwardness, and probably that was the case with Jesus.

However, dinner in Jesus' day was of more central importance than in our time. In ancient times it was understood that sharing a meal created, or cemented, a relationship. Thus, it mattered with whom you broke bread."[2]

Often in our scriptural interpretations we miss significant points such as when an unclean woman interrupts a meal in the Pharisee Simon's house; we understand the spiritual lessons of her actions but miss her personal depth of faith, and courage as she breaks cultural and social bounds that warmed Jesus' heart.

Before we continue, let it be noted that Jesus' followers would not of their own initiative have shared meals Jesus introduced them to. Yet it is no stretch of the imagination to understand Peter and the other disciple's hesitancy to associate meals with Gentiles, for they would never have contemplated such if not for following Jesus.

Elizabeth Schussler-Fiorenza writes "Christian meals are eating together, sharing together, drinking together, talking with each other, receiving from each other, experiencing God's presence through each other. And in so doing, proclaiming the gospel as God's alternative vision for everyone, especially for those who are poor, outcast, and battered."3

Luke records the early Church's understanding of this concept: "They followed a daily discipline of worship in the Temple followed by meals at home, every meal a celebration, exuberant and joyful as they praised God."   -Acts 2:46 {Message}

While I was preparing this manuscript for my editor my 10-year-old laptop gave up the ghost, and I was told I needed a new computer. During this down time, I received a notice from the library that a reserved book I had forgotten about, was available. Since it would be a few days before I got back online, I picked up the book, and to my delight it was *Dinner with the President*. The author, Alex Pru'Homme, weaves stories of 26 presidents' appetites showing how food is not just fuel when it is served to the most powerful people in the world, but a tool of communication, a lever of power and persuasion, a form of entertainment and a symbol of a nation.

What a timely interruption in my writing. While reading this book I was reminded of John 12:42 where we are told many of Israel's rulers came to believe in Jesus. I pondered how many of those believers had shared a table with Jesus.

A few years ago, all our kids and most of our grandkids came to visit us and helped celebrate my 70th birthday. As I watched the family playing, eating and laughing the power of "table talk" was being displayed before my eyes. That power was reminiscent of the power Jesus used in His ministry. It is my hope that as you read this book your own memories may reappear and inspire opportunities to be like Jesus during your dinner.

As we walk through dinner examples with Jesus, make it a goal to seek application, affirmation, challenge or correction. Look for a single discipline that you might be inspired to incorporate at your table.

Be Blessed – Timm Oyer

1. Totenberg, Nina, *Dinner with Ruth,* pg 183, Simon & Schuster, New York, NY.
2. Campbell, Cynthia, *Meeting Jesus at the Table,* page 20
3. Schussler-Fiorenza, Elizabeth

Chapter One

Early in Jesus' ministry, after choosing six followers, Jesus invites another, Matthew to follow Him. This was a life changing event in Matthew's life, and he wanted to share it with his friends. Prior to the invitation Matthew had been a despised tax collector, lacking hope, but when Jesus called him, he was amazingly changed, and Matthew couldn't wait to invite his tax collecting friends to meet Jesus.

"That night Matthew invited Jesus and His followers to be His dinner guests, along with his fellow tax collectors and many other notorious sinners. The Pharisees were indignant, 'why does your teacher eat with such scum they asked His disciples?'"
 -Matthew 9:10-11

It is important to remember, in ancient Jewish culture, bonds were made, and walls broken down at the table, and this was Matthew's intent in having a banquet.

"That night Matthew invited Jesus and His disciples to be his dinner guests, along with his

fellow tax collectors and many other notorious sinners." -Mark 2:15

Matthew was so overwhelmed with the grace Jesus showed him. Always aware of his past, there was no cost, no social barrier too prohibitive to invite his friends to meet his new Master and share a life-changing experience. Rarely have I envisioned dinner as a life-changing experience for those I have invited.

"Soon Matthew held a banquet in his home with Jesus as the guest of honor. Many of Matthew's fellow tax collectors and other guests were there." -Luke 5:29

As I read the story of Matthew's call to follow Jesus, I wonder at the mindset of the prior six disciples Jesus had called to follow Him. Until Matthew was chosen, Peter, James, John, Andrew, Philip and Nathaniel were all fishermen and Jesus had called them to be "fishers of men." One doubts any of them thought about becoming a friend of a tax-collector, so sitting at dinner in Matthew's house must have been a mind-boggling experience.

While being interviewed for a Podcast to promote this book, my friend Jane asked; "have you ever invited someone you barely knew to dinner?" I said "no, but my wife frequently does that." Think about this for a moment. Jesus tells the disciples He has chosen thus far that they are going to a tax collectors house for dinner! I would have loved to have been inside Peter's mind when he heard that. Fishermen invited to a tax collectors house, what in the world was Jesus' thinking? Then there was Matthew's friends, fellow tax collectors, just a half-step above lepers on the social ladder and never allowed to go inside a synagogue, being told by Matthew he was going to give up his vocation to follow this young rabbi.

What lesson was to be learned in this unusual table experience. What did it have to do with fishing for men? Have you ever wondered why Christ is asking you to invite someone with whom you have nothing in common to your table?

Luke's use of the word "banquet" indicates it was a dinner that was more than just a small affair. Being a Gentile, Luke refuses to use the word "sinners" to identify Matthews guests.

Numerous times in my pastoral ministry, especially at church potlucks, someone would caution me not to partake from someone's dish for a supposed health reason. As a result, I would make sure I didn't. After one such occasion my wife was remarking on how delicious a dish was and asked if I had any to eat. When I told her that someone had advised me against it, she informed me that the individual whose advice I followed had a strong prejudice against that person. From that experience I learned to take others' opinions with greater care.

The table is not only a place of fellowship, and affirmation, but also an occasion for new fellowship. The Table is for mending brokenness and facilitating forgiveness. And more importantly as Matthew exhibited, a place for introducing friends to Jesus.

My aunt Kitty's table was ladened with delicious food for Sunday dinners! She and Uncle Kent made sure favorites were prepared for family and friends. It was a treat to be included at their dinner table! The beauty of their home and hospitality was not in the furnishings or food, but their habit of always inviting new people to join the meal, just like Jesus.3

......Centered Prayer ......

Father, help me to see others through Your eyes. Teach me to look past the outward appearance to recognize future possibilities. Remind me, as You did the prophet, of the pit which I dug. It may be true that my pit was not as deep or evil as someone else's pit, but I was just as stuck until You came to lift me out.

Help me to offer the mercy I received. Help me to share the grace I have been shown. Burden me with the desire to lead others to You. May Your Spirit give me insight into how to be a witness to those who may appear to be very different than I am. In a society that has become increasingly skeptical, give me wisdom to speak Your truth in love. Let me see through Your eyes, reach out of Your heart, show compassion to the same measure I have been given. Amen

3.Ministry Illustration, Sherry Oyer, *Champaign, Illinois*

CHAPTER RELECTION ... Matthew

Have you ever been excited about inviting someone to your house for a meal for the first time?

Have you been afraid to invite someone because of what others might think about you?

My reflections on how this chapter spoke to me.

My Notes

Chapter Two

"The next day Jesus' mother was a guest at a wedding celebration in the village of Cana of Galilee. Jesus and His disciples were also invited to the celebration."

-John 2:1-2

One of the most important days in the life of a Jewish male was his wedding day. Prior to his marriage, the groom would spend a year preparing a house for his bride. The house was usually close to the groom's father's home. The groom would also lay aside a sum of money if his wife was to become a wife, he would brag about at the city gates. [Proverbs 31:28]. It was a part of his responsibility to provide her with a financial base on which she could build. Jesus notes in John's gospel, that He has gone to prepare a place for His bride, His Church, at His Father's place.

For Jesus' mother Mary the wedding feast at Cana was that special family gathering where the Spirit spoke to her and was the first time for Jesus' intercession. At the wedding, the bridal party ran out of wine for their guests. Mary had no idea how Jesus would fix the situation, nor did she need to know. She simply told the servants to do as He told them. Exemplifying faith supreme, no questions, no doubts, just "do it" attitude. [John 2:5]

We are fond of this story because it is the first of Jesus of many miracles; and the miracle happens at the table. Turning the water into wine was a great first miracle. Even greater was the fact Jesus was sparing that young groom from a very embarrassing time. At a wedding feast the best wine was served first, then as the party continued and guests became more intoxicated the lesser wine was usually served. But Jesus turned the tables and the wine He offered towards the end of the wedding celebration was the finest ever.

It is no coincidence that Jesus' first miracle is about wine. At the last supper Jesus tells His disciples He will not share it again until that great Lamb's Wedding Feast in heaven.

When planning a special table time everything from seating to napkin folding deserves special attention. Everything should say to the guests "this is for you." I think of a men's prayer breakfast I attended where my friend, Brian, would begin preparation at home the night before. Then in the morning he would bring the ingredients, even the condiments which the church provided, nothing was left to chance, the smallest detail not forgotten.

I can always predict when one of our kids is coming to visit! Shopping and ingredients are gathered, special baking and cooking is started, it's a big deal, not the usual time of a casual meal.

My wife was impressed with a restaurant in Disneyland's Magic Kingdom that had the motto "Be Our Guest," taken from the song titled the same. Some lyrics go like this *"Be our guest, be our guest. Put our service to the test. We only live to serve."*[4]

During the Christmas holiday one year we were invited to dinner by friends in our church. Their farmhouse was a long way from the main highway, with no neighbors in sight! Even so, as we approached their home it was beautifully beaming with lights and Christmas decorations. We were seated at a beautifully set table while dining on several of their family favorite dishes. The warmth and love shared around that table was amazing.[5]

Oh, that the guests at my table may sense that their hearts are strangely drawn closer to the Lord.

As I reflect on the thirty years of Jesus' preparation, the hours of Brians attention to detail, the restaurant's goal, and the candlelit holiday dinner in the country, the usual hassle of seemingly trivial things gain significance. I am assured that the wedding feast in heaven will far exceed anything I can imagine.

......*Centered Prayer*......

Father, heaven will be a more beautiful place than my greatest imagination. The promise that no eye has seen, nor ear has heard, nor has it entered my heart what You have prepared, gets me excited. I am humbled to realize You care so much for Your creation that a place like that is being prepared for us.
You also said no unclean thing will enter that place. So, teach me to walk in unison with Your Spirit so I will not gratify the desires of flesh and corrupt my soul.

Remind me because I committed to consider myself dead to sin, I no longer have any right to live with the habits from which I was delivered. Show me the door of escape You have provided for every temptation the enemy can send my way. Help me to disciplined Kingdom living so when I get there it will feel just like home.

4. Oyer, Sherry, *Be Our Guest Restaurant, Disney World Resort, Orlando, Florida*
5. Ministry Illustration, Oyer, Sherry, *Champaign, Illinois*

CHAPTER REFLECTION ... CANA

HAVE YOU EVER SHARED WITH YOUR TABLE GUESTS HOW GOD HAS HELPED YOU PREPARE FOR THE MEAL?

HAVE YOU EVER INVITED A SPECIAL FRIEND TO A MEAL BECAUSE OF THEIR SPIRITUAL INFLUENCE?

WHAT MESSAGE DOES MARY'S REQUEST OF JESUS IMPLY TO YOU?

MY NOTES

Chapter Three

"When Jesus arrived at Peter's house Peter's mother-in-law was in bed with a high fever. But when Jesus touched her hand, the fever left her. Then she got up and prepared a meal for Him."
-Matthew 8:14-15

"Jesus went to her bedside, and He took her by the hand and helped her sit up, and the fever suddenly left, and she got up and prepared a meal for them."

Mark 1:31
"Standing by her bedside He spoke to the fever, rebuking it, and immediately her temperature returned to normal. She got up at once and prepared a meal for them."
-Luke 4:39

Matthew, Mark and Luke record Jesus' visit to Peter's Mother-in-Law, who was suffering with sickness. Jesus arrives and rebukes her fever. Once the fever left Peter's Mother-in-Law, she got busy and prepared a meal for Jesus.

It is amazing that strength and health were restored to that woman immediately. There was no need for time to recover, no need for strength to gather. She is miraculously completely healed and went to work immediately and fixed them a meal.

"What can I offer the Lord for all He has done for me? I will lift a cup symbolizing His salvation; I will praise the Lord's name for saving me." Psalm 116:12

What a testimony Peter's Mother-in-Law's meal was. The meal wasn't insignificant - it was inspirational. The verb Mark uses to describe the woman's "serving" is the same word to describe Jesus' table ministry. Have you ever wondered, what aside from her healing, leads Peter's Mother-in-Law to the kitchen? Is she responding to the voice of the Spirit or doing what seems the natural thing to do to say thank you.

In the flow of servanthood from Jesus to the woman and from the woman back to Jesus I want my table ministry to be the same. I want my table talk to always be a testimony of Christs love for me and those with whom I dine. May all who leave my table feel spiritually refreshed.

……. Centered Prayer……

"Father, my reaction to your grace is important. I confess that I am tempted to be a consumer of your blessings and not take the time to share them. Forgive me for that offense to Your love. My greatest value as a believer in this lost world is what I gave, not in what I accumulate. This is true in both a spiritual and physical sense.

Help me to develop a servant's heart and a generous nature. I can't do everything, but I can do something that offers the divine compassion and hospitality of your family.

Bring conviction to my life when I make excuses for not doing what I know I should. Every time I see a table may I be reminded I am looking at a special tool by which to share life with someone else.   Amen

CHAPTER RELECTION... PETER'S MOTHER-IN-LAW

HAVE YOU EVER CONSIDERED A MEAL A HEALING OCCASION?

**WHAT DOES THIS WOMAN'S IMMEDIATELY FIXING A MEAL SAY
ABOUT HER CHARACTER?**

**COULD PREPARING A MEAL FOR SOMEONE BE AN OCCASION TO
CELEBRATE A HEALING?**

MY NOTES

Chapter Four

"Jesus told the people to sit down on the grass. And He took the five loaves and two fish, looked up towards heaven and asked God's blessing on the food. Breaking the loaves into pieces, He gave some of the bread and fish to each disciple, and the disciples gave them to the people. They all ate as much as they wanted, and the disciples picked twelve baskets of leftovers."
 -Matthew 14:13-21; Mark 6:30-44; Luke 9:10-17; John 6:1-144 (Feeding the 4000 – Matthew 15:29-39)

Mark and Luke's gospels tell us the people sat in groups of fifty on the hillside. They gathered because word of Jesus' healing and miracle powers had drawn them. John's gospel tells us there were 5000 men, women and children. This would be a good day's work of serving and collecting for the disciples.

John tells us Jesus takes a young boy's lunch, consisting of five loaves and two fish the size of sardines and Jesus multiplies the lunch to feed the multitudes. As many times as I have taught this story the meager quality of this lunch never struck me. Yet this boy leaves home that morning with a lunch that will feed thousands. Many of the people had second helpings before the disciples picked up the leftovers. What a story they had to tell the rest of their lives!

The Master of the Universe chose to serve this poor boy's lunch to show He can take our meager offerings and turn them into a gift that glorifies Him and outlasts our expectations. There is always plenty when God is present.

One day at a funeral meal the head hostess approached me and said "Pastor there are many more than expected and we don't have enough to feed everyone, what do we do? I replied, WE PRAY!" God multiplied that mac and cheese and meatballs as only HE could and each person, including the helpers, were fed!6 '

Chuck Colson, founder of Prison Fellowship, told a story about how God can do wonderful things through the faithfulness of people we might ignore. He and his team did a seminar in prison which included preaching, a reformed inmate's testimony, and a famed gospel singer sharing the gift of song. At the end of several days of the seminar, one inmate stood up to thank Mr. Colson for his team's ministry. But the inmate wasn't grateful for what we might have expected. He said he appreciated all that had been done, but what really impacted him was that the ladies on the team came in after the program ended and sat down to eat with the inmates. This man said these women's actions changed his view of Christ more than anything else he experienced. 7

Just as God was present in the feeding of the 5,000, in the ministry in that prison, He wants to be invited to our table!

.......Centered Prayer.......

"Father, sometimes I see how small the things I hold in my hands seem to be. I stop before I ever start because what I have seems so little. I forget too often what You can do with my 'little.' You are a miracle working God.

Remind me that the small things in my hand are great when I give them to you. It is true that little is much when You are in it.

I must confess there are times I echo the words of the Roman official who said, 'I believe, help my unbelief.' The world around me often clouds my eyes from seeing through the lens of faith. Forgive me when I doubted Your leading when I was aware of Your Will. Forgive me for doubting when it seemed I held so little.

Teach me to believe in great things, give me a glimpse into what can be before it comes to pass. Give me eyes to see possibilities where others see the obstacles. Amen

6. Oyer, Timm, *Hastings Church of Nazarene, Hastings Michigan*
7. Goettsche, Bruce, *Feeding the Multitude – Luke 9"10-17*, Sermon

CHAPTER 4 REFLECTIONS 5,000

ARE THERE TIMES YOU HAVE BEEN IMPRESSED TO INVITE SOMEONE FOR A MEAL, BUT BEEN TOO INTIMIDATED TO DO SO?

WHAT HAVE YOU LEARNED IN THIS CHAPTER THAT ENCOURAGES YOU TO REACH OUT?

WHAT ENCOURAGES YOU ABOUT THE LITTLE BOYS' FAITH? COULD HE HAVE POSSIBLY THOUGHT HIS LUNCH COULD FEED 5,000 PEOPLE?

My Notes

Chapter Five

"So, when the Samaritans came to Him, they were asking Jesus to stay with them; and He stayed there two days"   *-John 4:40*

This story begins with Jesus resting at the Well of Jacob in Samaria. He had sent the disciples into the town of Sychar to get food. While Jesus is there a woman from the village approaches the well. This is a highly unusual situation. The woman had come at an unusual hour because she was a cast off in the city. This is a meeting between a Samaritan woman and a Jewish man. Jesus asks her for a drink of water and a conversation starts.

This gospel story includes one of the lengthiest conversations Jesus has with this woman, yet it is extremely lacking in detail about Jesus and the disciples stay with the people of Sychar. The fact that Jesus chose to stay in Sychar must have confused the disciples. A very radical Rabbi Eliezer, who briefly followed Jesus, told his Jewish followers "That one who breaks bread with the Samaritans eats the flesh of swine."

Where the disciples saw only a brief rest stop in a despised country Jesus saw a field of harvest for the gospel message. This tells us that regardless of the perceived social/cultural status of any guest at my table I must see them through Christ eyes. It also reminds me that the table can be a place of testimony and opportunity to praise God. The fact that the Samaritan woman's testimony was even listened to let alone accepted, gives evidence of the Spirits power to persuade in the simplest of praise.

After the conversation with Jesus this woman is so changed that she shares with her towns people who had not been accepting of her, that she had met the Messiah. May those who share at my table leave feeling it has been a wholesome experience as it did with the woman at the well.

When the Apostle Paul confronts Peter about his reluctance to eat with Gentiles [Gal. 2:11-13] one wonders if memories of Peter's experience in Sychar enter his mind. As the disciples spread throughout the world to share the gospel, one wonders what influence those few days in Samaria continued to have, and the fruitfulness of the woman's testimony to them!

This story inspires me to always remember food is a vessel through which the Spirit provides nourishment of the soul!

.......Centered Prayer.......

"Father, guard me from hesitating to minister to someone because of where they are from. I reject the notion that there is any place in my life for prejudice or being judgmental because of a person's birth circumstances.
Teach me to look beyond what the world would say is unclean and unacceptable. May my spirit not be plagued with any attitude of thinking that I am superior to anyone else. Help me to resist the temptation that comes when I need to approach someone who has a tarnished reputation or seems to be unapproachable.

Remind me that You created everything, and I am not to call any part of Your creation unclean. Open my mind to the incredible possibilities found when You come to bring life to a person. May I be the first to offer grace and a path to new life in Christ. Fill my heart and my words with the passion of Your love. Help me to invite the "unclean" to a table of fellowship and offer hope to a hungry soul. Amen.

CHAPTER 5 REFLECTIONS

DO I PREFER TO HAVE MEALS ONLY WITH PEOPLE I AM COMFORTABLE WITH?

DO I "INTENTIONALLY" INVITE PEOPLE TO A MEAL SO I CAN SHARE WHAT GOD IS DOING IN MY LIFE?

IS THERE A SENSE AT MY TABLE THAT IT'S OKAY TO SHARE INTIMATE FEELINGS?

MY NOTES

Chapter Six

"And it came about when Jesus went into the house of one of the leaders of the Pharisees on the Sabbath to eat bread that they were watching Him closely."

Luke 14:1-24

Talk about eating at a hostile table!

I am certainly not inclined to dine with those who vigorously oppose me, but then I am not Jesus. At the meal there are no disciples present. Scholars tell us that it is a meal where only "prestigious leaders" of the Jewish faith are invited, and a lame man, who is to serves as bait for Jesus. I am sure Jesus is aware of this.

There are a few lessons to be learned from Jesus' example in accepting His invitation. First, it is not right to turn down a table invitation because of a prejudice, opposition, or fear of being outnumbered. If I believe God controls every aspect of my life, and I do, He has chosen the invitation and there is a lesson to be gained from the experience that will glorify Him. Remember, Jesus washed Judas' feet and shared communion with him knowing Judas was going to betray Him.

Secondly, recognize that though there may be a trap set for me, as the lame man was for Jesus, God has every intention of using it.

Remember when Joseph's brothers realized it was their brother, they sold into slavery who had the power to say whether they would receive the life-saving grain their families needed. Joseph told them "You intended to harm me, but God intended it for good and the preservation of many people." {Genesis 45} God may intend for me be invited to a hostile table so that He may be glorified.

I wonder where Jesus was seated at the table. Was it in a place where everyone could easily see and hear Him? I am certain He wasn't the guest of honor. Is there a prejudice or pecking order at my table?

The author of *"Dinner with the President"* tells us that at state dinners many presidents seated guests at round tables to facilitate conversation and provide a sense of equality important at a President's table.

.....Centered Prayer.....

Father, help me to remember You have called me to set an example. It is not comfortable to know others are always watching to see if I live up to my Christian profession of faith. Remind me often that You did not call me to be comfortable but to be salt and light.

May I be anointed with the ability to be salt by adding value to the multitude of conversations around the host of tables I will be honored to sit at during my life.

May I accept the responsibility to be light showing others the way to You and the salvation You offer. Move me out of my comfort zone so I can be a greater witness. May I recognize the opportunities You have ordained at every table where I am invited to sit.

Take away the anxiety of the uncomfortable with the knowledge of these moments great purpose.
—Amen

CHAPTER 6 REFLECTIONS

ARE YOU EVER TEMPTED TO INVITE SOMEONE TO A MEAL TO PROMOTE YOURSELF OR TO EXPRESS A PERSONAL VIEW?

WHAT SHOULD OUR MOTIVE[S] BE FOR INVITING SOMEONE TO SHARE AT OUR TABLE?

CAN EVEN A NONBELIEVER FIND REFUGE AT YOUR TABLE, OR INSPIRATION TO CONSIDER GOD?

MY NOTES

Chapter Seven

"When Jesus came by, He looked up at Zacchaeus and called him by name. 'Zacchaeus!' He said 'quick, come down, for I must be a guest in your home today.'"   *-Luke 19:1-10*

Jesus is on His way with His disciples to Jerusalem during holy week. This story is an interruption in their journey, it is intentional. Jesus intends to invite Himself to Zacchaeus house, and Zacchaeus has every intention of seeing Jesus. Being the CEO of the Regional Roman Tax Collection Division Zacchaeus does not want to standout, but he had to see Jesus. Zacchaeus is very short and believe me there is no self-respecting Jew that is going to let him sit on their shoulders! How often in life do we want to be favorably seen by Jesus, but not to the extent we are confronted by His will?

Remember that Sunday School song:
   Zacchaeus was a Wee little man,
   A Wee little man was he
   He climbed up in the Sycamore tree
   For the Lord he wanted to see!

Luke tells us that there were two cultural obstacles broken by Zacchaeus that he might see Jesus. First, no self-respecting Jewish man would run – Zacchaeus ran! Second, no Jewish man would climb a tree – Zacchaeus climbed! These actions tell me that Zacchaeus, with his wealth and power, knew he had a hunger that only Jesus could fill.

Have you ever timidly invited someone to your table, and their excited acceptance of your invitation shocked you? On Jesus part, He intentionally stops and looks Zacchaeus in the eye, and intentionally invites Himself to Zacchaeus's house for dinner. We often short-change Jesus when limiting ourselves to only inviting guests with whom we feel comfortable with.

This was better than Zacchaeus could have dreamed, he was going to host Jesus. When I am challenged to host someone that I wouldn't on my own invite, there isn't excitement, but healthy anticipation of what might be. There are times in my life when despite my happy preparations, the Holy Spirit has plans that surpass anything I can imagine.

By virtue of the story, it must have made a grand meal richer by his sharing with Jesus. The most ordinary meal becomes more satisfying when Christ is invited into the conversation.

......Centered Prayer ....

Father, I am surrounded by people like Zacchaeus and often forget it. I rub elbows each day with people who are curious as well as those who are genuinely seeking for truth. I have failed in recognizing the opportunity to witness because of my busy-ness. I have too often rushed right by them. I have neglected to hear the cry of a seeking heart because I did not take the time to really listen. I have been far too intent on getting someone to understand me instead of working hard to understand them.

Knowledge means nothing if I am not hearing the real questions. I pray for discernment to listen to what people are really asking. Teach me to hold my tongue until I know their questions. Forgive me for my past failures and help me not miss another Zacchaeus that crosses my path. Help me to become the beacon which calls the lost person to safe harbor. Amen

CHAPTER 7 REFLECTIONS

IF SOMEONE INVITED THEMSELVES TO YOUR HOUSE, OR STRONGLY SUGGESTED THEY WOULD LIKE TO EAT WITH YOU, WHAT WOULD YOUR IMMEDIATE RESPONSE BE?

WHEN YOU INVITE SOMEONE TO YOUR TABLE WHAT ARE YOU EXPECTING?

WHAT IS THE MOST UNEXPECTED BUT GREATEST CHANGE IN YOUR LIFE BECAUSE OF A GUEST VISIT AT YOUR TABLE?

MY NOTES:

Chapter Eight

As Jesus and His disciples continued their way to Jerusalem, they came to a village where a woman named Martha invited them into their home. Her sister, Mary, sat at Jesus' feet listening to what He taught. But Martha was worrying over the big dinner she was preparing. —
Luke 10:38-42

Scholars tell us that in Jesus' day, there was an open invitation for Him at Lazarus' house. Remember, Lazarus was a close friend of Jesus. It was Lazarus whose death Jesus wept over. When Jesus was in the area He was expected to stop and share a meal with Lazarus and his sisters Martha and Mary.

Shortly after Sherry and I were married I took her to meet close relatives of mine, she asked if we shouldn't call ahead, and I said "nope, I have an open invitation". Upon arriving, without knocking on the front door, I ushered her into a generous welcome. She told me later she was so impressed that they were genuinely happy we stopped by! Such was the welcome Jesus experienced at His friends' home.

Martha in her excitement of Jesus coming, is laboring in the kitchen. This meal is special because Jesus is coming, but Mary goes with Him into the living room to talk and sit at His feet.

Martha is no less excited that Jesus is in their home than her younger sister, just distracted [v.39]. Luke tells us the meal was not only special but big. And sometimes the importance of the ingredients, or rush of the meal, distracts from the goal of the meal.

There are times when the importance of a guest, or the immediacy of an issue delay the spreading of praise or the good news, and it is not until after a meal we realize the true goal was never met. We are always waiting for that special moment, and in our timing miss it completely. Note that in Jesus' reply to Martha's concern He does not chastise or criticize just patiently corrects her. [vs.41-42]

In Martha's desire for that perfect dinner, she loses sight of the spiritual importance her guest was sharing. How often have we been distracted by our worry about everything going according to plan. Whenever the social importance of my meal takes over the spiritual significance my plans are useless.

One wonders how many times in Jesus' sharing were others more concerned about preparations than what Jesus had to share?

.......Centered Prayer.......

Father, teach me to set the proper priorities in life. May the urgent never distract me from the necessary. Help me not to miss the moments You have prepared to spend with me because I could not get my mind off the next event or responsibility.

I am reminded in this story that it was not an issue of right and wrong, but of what's best. The important things can wait when the imperative takes precedence. Dinner can wait another hour, if it is time to sit with the Master.

I confess I have missed opportunities to draw up close to You because I have allowed the urgent to rule my life. Over the years I realized the urgent will always be with me, I need to recognize the moments I need to stop and just be with You. Teach me to recognize when You have led me to a spiritual oasis in the middle of this overly busy life.   Amen

CHAPTER 8 REFLECTIONS

DOES MY TABLE TALK FOCUS MORE OR LESS ON OTHER TOPICS THAN OF SHARING ABOUT THE GOODNESS OF CHRIST?

SUM UP IN SENTENCES HOW BOTH MARY AND MARTHA RELATE TO YOU?

MY NOTES

Chapter Nine

Jesus said, "I have looked forward to this hour with deep longing, anxious to eat this Passover meal with you before my suffering begins. For I tell you now I won't eat it again until it comes to fulfillment in the Kingdom of God."
Luke 22:15-16

I like Rev. Carl Leth's definition of the Last Supper: "Food for the Journey." The journey to the Garden of Gethsemane, the journey to His beatings. The journey to the cross. The journey to the grave and the journey concluding in His Resurrection!"[9]

For the last ten years of my ministry on Maundy Thursday I would prepare a Passover meal for all the congregants that would attend. We would go through the meal as though we were back in biblical times. In the Passover meal four cups are celebrated [in order: Sanctification, deliverance, redemption and praise] and when we came to the third cup, the cup of redemption or salvation, we celebrated Communion just as Jesus did. To those participating in the Passover meal the tradition brought the Old Testament to fulfillment in the New.

We are all familiar with Da Vinci's painting of the Last supper, and though it is beautiful, it is tragically flawed. Jewish meals were generally eaten sitting on cushions in a circle on the floor, but the Pharisees had ruled that during Passover they were to sit on chairs around U-shaped tables. Hence at the Last Supper the person on Jesus' right was his most trusted friend, that position He gave to John. To His left, the most honored position, He gave to Judas. To the extreme left, the servant's place, Peter sat, not because he was the humblest, but possibly because he expected Jesus to ask him to sit closer.

How often at the arranging of our table do we seat people according to their supposed social standing, financial welfare or achievements? Have you noted that an individual who always waits until everyone is seated then takes the place furthest away on purpose, faking humility. That was Peter. Tragically even after Jesus serves them some argued about who was greater among themselves.

As meal preparations are important to selecting the right foods, drinks, etc. so it is just as important to make sure no one is intentionally seated at our table in any place of hindrance. If there is a place of difficulty it should be occupied by the host, not a guest. A place at the table should always be a special place where everyone can find connection and feel a part of the meal.

Jesus chose to give Judas a place of honor at the Last Supper. It was another intentional way of offering Judas grace, mercy and a chance to change. Our table should offer the same range of options to every guest at our table!

…..Centered Prayer ……

Father, I acknowledge how I treat, and respect others is important to You. I am not telling You something but reminding myself that You instructed me to treat others as I would like to be treated. There is no place this becomes more obvious than when people come together as a group.

There is always a temptation to place people according to a worldly view of importance and value. Guard my heart from placing others in classes or categories. Remind me to show others a place honor and me sit in the lesser seat. Teach me to look for the seat of a servant, a place to learn and gain more of the heart Christ.

Let me sit in the lesser place with as much joy as any place of honor could afford. Never let me do this with some underlying pride but with authenticity. preferring others above myself. May I honor You with a servant's heart. Amen

8. Leth, Carl, *Holiness Today, January/February 2021, page 18*

CHAPTER 9 REFLECTIONS

HAVE YOU EVER DONE SOMETHING TOTALLY DIFFERENT AT THE TABLE THAT SURPRISED EVERYONE?

HAS ANYONE EVER REMARKED ABOUT HOW BLESSED THEY FELT WHILE SHARING A MEAL WITH YOU?

MY NOTES

Chapter Ten

"By this time, they were nearing Emmaus and the end of their journey. Jesus would have gone on, but they begged him spend the night with them, since it was getting late. So, He went with them. As they sat down to eat, He took a small loaf of bread, asked God's blessing on it, broke it, then gave it to them. Suddenly their eyes were opened, and they recognized him."

-Luke 24:13-32

No fantastic miracles, no great signs of wonder, just a simple breaking of the bread! Scholars tell us the disciples saw the nail prints in Jesus' hands and recognized Him. I want to present a different view.

As the disciples began to review their journey from Jerusalem, they recalled that as Jesus opened scripture to them their hearts began to burn. Have there been times in your life when listening to someone explaining scripture, or just reading scripture yourself, or during a sermon, you experienced a strange warming of your heart? The "burning" was the Spirit's way of preparing them, and you at times, for seeing the resurrected Christ among them.

Have you ever had something you are looking for right in front of you and can't see it? How often we are told by religious leaders "God is with you, He never leaves." King David tells us "The Lord will watch over our coming and going both now and forevermore." [Psalm 121:8]

Wise advice says:

> When you can't see Jesus,
> When you can't hear Jesus,
> Look to the scriptures!

Do you ever wonder why the Spirit is urging you to invite someone with whom you have nothing in common to your table? Maybe that individual is the Spirit in disguise, or through that guest the Spirit has something to reveal to you. We are encouraged in scripture *"Don't forget to show hospitality to strangers, for some who have done this have entertained angels without realizing it."* [Hebrews 13:2]

Remember an ah-hah moment when something entered your mind that you knew didn't originate with you, despite it seeming familiar? It's at that moment, the nail print in His hands, the breaking of the bread – the same way Jesus had broken the bread for the 5,000 feeding and at the Last Supper, their eyes were opened! Remember when your guest said or did something, and a light switched on?

At the table as we engage in conversation, and become more personal, our hearts become warmed, approaching that moment of unexpected revelation. In this sense my mind goes back to the time Jesus spoke with the Samaritan woman, and the longer Jesus spoke the more she desired to hear from Him.

While in my last year at Olivet Nazarene University my wife and I were invited, along with fellow classmates, to dinner at our professor's house. During the meal and table talk, I mentioned how impressed I was with the drinking water. As you may have guessed, there was a brief period of silence and weird looks from others at the table. Professor Woodruff mentioned his family's pride in the artisan well in their backyard! My hometown, Montpelier, Ohio has for many years won an International World Water Tasting Contest. I have oft times shared that information. Our professor realized my observation was an opportunity for him to share that the water was cool and refreshing without an added purifying ingredient!

Allow me to conclude with a lesson this story has taught me. Spiritual brokenness is not a negative thing, it's an invitation to wholeness, to new growth! Table talks with Jesus are always warming.

......Centered Prayer......

Father, too many special God moments have passed by because I was distracted by the complexities of daily life. I should have recognized how You were moving. I have missed Emmaus Road experiences that have come my way. Forgive my rushing through life. When I have been paying attention, those moments were so precious they are marked on the calendar of my life. I believe You still have many heart-warming life encounters for my life.

Teach me to quiet my spirit so I may hear the voice of Your Spirit speaking. Remind me to slow down as I walk through the crowds because it is in community that we often get to experience these moments. I confess I have often been so focused on the destination I missed the joy of the journey.

Slow my steps when I walk among Your people. Soften my heart so the warming presence of Your Spirit may burst into a flame with my heart.
Amen

Chapter 10 Reflections

HAVE YOU EXPERIENCED A "HEART WARMING" TIME AT A MEAL?

HAVE YOU EVER ALLOWED A NEGATIVE STATEMENT TO BECOME A GROWTH EXPERIENCE?

HAS A GUEST EVER TOLD OF AN "AH-HAH' MOMENT?

MY NOTES

Chapter Eleven

"Still later He appeared to the eleven disciples as they were eating together."

-Mark 16:14

And just as they were telling about it [the two from Emmaus] Jesus Himself was suddenly among them. The whole group was terribly frightened, thinking they were seeing a ghost! Jesus asked them: Do you have something to eat?" They gave him a piece of boiled fish, and He ate it as they watched Him."

-Luke 24:35

This is the most difficult, and frustrating chapter of this book for me to pen and grapple with. The disciples heard the witness of the women, the witness of the empty tomb from John and Peter, and now they are hearing pretty much the same witness from these followers from Emmaus, and they are still locked behind closed doors.

Sadly, the most likely conclusion I can come up with is that their minds are like those on the road to Emmaus; focused on the betrayal in the garden, a broken Jesus dying on the cross. And now someone had stolen His body, their humanness completely blocking out who Jesus was. To me it's as though they have forgotten He is THE Son of God! Yet I must confess there are times in my life where my focus on immediate circumstances blinds my faith.

"The degree to which we are tied to this world greatly influences our ability to see, trust, and obey the Holy Spirit. Often despite spiritual encouragement from brothers and sisters in Christ!"

Then Jesus challenges them to see, and feel, the nail prints in His feet and hands, and touch the wound in His side [John 20:26]. I can relate. We are all quicker to accept that which we can see and feel, yet He takes it a step further and asks for food. Now it gets interesting! First a resurrected body does not need earthly food, and second, once again He has appeared at the table.

I am reminded that most of Jesus disciples are fishermen. Perhaps there are some memories that Jesus is using? In attempting to connect the eating of fish with Jesus' appearance I am reminded that in those times when I am tempted to worry, times of Christ past faithfulness, flash across my mind and urge me to call on Him.

......Centered Prayer.......

Father, this is a busy life I lead. It seems as if there is never enough time to accomplish all there is to do. I recognize that is what the enemy wants to create in my life. However, when I stop and look, I realize You have a unique opportunity to sit with others whether it be at a table or around a campfire.

You have most often spoken into my life when I have taken time to quiet my mind and slow down. May I learn to look at my "table moments" as a life necessity. May I realize the importance of spending time with You as well as spending time with others in community.

Teach me to anticipate You working in these moments, so I won't miss the blessing. Remind me of why I need to remove the distractions so my soul may be quieted. Let me become more and more sensitive to Your voice in my life. I truly want to follow the good Shepherd. I commit to making my table times opportunities to engage with You and with others a priority for Your glory and my spiritual health. -Amen

CHAPTER 11 REFLECTIONS

HAS SOMETHING A GUEST SAID AT MEALTIME INSPIRED YOUR FAITH?

HAVE YOU OFFERED HOPE TO A GUEST DURING MEALTIME?

MY NOTES

Chapter Twelve

Then the disciple whom Jesus loved said to Peter, "It is the Lord!" As soon as Simon Peter heard him say, "It is the Lord," he wrapped his outer garment around him and jumped into the water. The other disciples followed in the boat, towing the net full of fish, for they were not far from shore, about a hundred yards. When they landed, they saw a fire with burning coal and fish on it, and some bread.
—John 21:1-14

These verses illustrate why Peter is my favorite Bible character. He jumps out of the boat! I admit after doing it once and sinking I doubt I would try it again. But having walked on water once Peter knows all he needs to do to get to Jesus is to keep focused on Him.

"Is there any bigger discipline in our spiritual journey than to 'stay focused on Christ?'"

It is also amazing to me that Peter doesn't recognize Jesus' voice, but he hears John say that it is and that is enough. There are times at the table when Jesus speaks through a guest's voice, and this is why listening at the table is so crucial!

In the prior chapter I talked about the Professor realizing the moment when he could share after my comment about the quality of their water; this story reminds me that the Professor was listening, or was the Spirit urging him to share?

We note in the story that Jesus has prepared breakfast, a breakfast fishermen would be used to. He then invited the disciples to join Him and add some from their catch. We hope that people feel excited about our invitation to our table, and even more excited when they are asked to contribute to it. In asking the disciples to contribute to the breakfast, Jesus is celebrating their obedience to His call to cast their nets again. Yes, I know that Peter was repentant, but I wonder if he didn't recall those marvelous moments journeying with Jesus? 9

Recently we were invited to spend the day with friends on their private beach front. It was a wonderful time in fellowship, and a casual gathering around the beach table for a delicious "shrimp boil". When asked, "what can we bring?" Our friend graciously let us know what was needed. As much as we enjoyed the boil it will always be the fellowship we remember.

My mother was always helping others but extremely reluctant to accept the offer of others to help her. One day as she was making an excuse of why I couldn't help I patiently asked her why she refused God's leading for help. She gave me a look of confusion. So, I asked her, "when you help others do you sense the Spirit encouraging you?" "Yes" she replied, then I asked, "have you ever stopped to think that when others want to help you, they are following the Spirits leading and receive encouragement."

Our invitation for a guest to bring a certain dish to our table recognizes their importance to our table. Not extending an offer can encourage mixed emotions or a sense of not being that worthy.

I cannot imagine the story of the young lad and his feelings every time in his life's journey he talked about Jesus multiplying his meager lunch – those were the lads' 5 loaves and 2 fishes multiplied beyond human imagination!

   Margaret Feinberg in her wonderful book "*Taste and See*" says "…. *the numbers five and two are important because together they add up to the perfect number seven, which symbolizes completeness, divine perfection throughout scripture.*"10

Are there times we don't invite others to bring a dish because of a prior negative whisper, or their dish may not meet our standards, OR the hidden fear they might receive more recognition?

.......Centered Prayer.......

Father, You instituted the first meal that had a real mission. This meal on the beach was to renew the call of each disciple, but especially Peter. Help me to learn from this example and go to the table with a mission. The first mission is to allow You to speak into my life. The second mission is to always go to the table with a heart to add value into the lives of others.

The mission may take many forms in differing setting, but the idea is always consistent to make each meal take on purpose. Help me not miss the moments You have to renew my spirit, to encourage my soul, and to renew the call You have placed on my life. Just as important may I facilitate the opportunity for others to experience the same blessing when they sit at the table with me. Remind me to live with purpose and for Your glory.   -Amen

9. Ministry Illustration, Oyer, Sherry, *Beach Party at the Portenga's,* Traverse City, Mi.
10. Feinberg, Margaret, *Taste and See, pg.87,* Harper Christian Resources Publisher

CHAPTER 12 REFLECTIONS

HAVE THERE BEEN TIMES IN MY LIFE, WHEN GOD HAS PERFORMED THE MIRACULOUS THAT I LOVE TO SHARE AT MEALTIME?

HAS THERE BEEN A TIME A GUEST HAS SHARED SOMETHING THAT MADE A LASTING IMPACT ON MY LIFE?

HAVE I EVER THOUGHT MY CONTRIBUTION IS TOO SMALL TO MAKE A DIFFERENCE, BUT GOD HAS INTERCEEDED?

MY NOTES

Heavens Wedding Banquet

The Lord of Host will prepare a lavish banquet for all people on this mountain; a banquet of rich food, a feast of seven courses, and refined, aged wine.
Isaiah 25:6

Jesus said, "I have looked forward to this hour with deep longing, anxious to eat this Passover meal with you before My sufferings begin. For I tell you now that I won't eat it again until it comes to fulfillment in the Kingdom of God."
Luke 22"15-16

"Let us be glad and rejoice and honor Him. For the time has come for the wedding feast of the Lamb, and His bride has prepared herself."
Revelation 19:7

The Lamb's Wedding Banquet! The Perfect Table! There is nothing human about its preparation and presentation. Nothing in human experience can approach one aspect of this meal.

The closest I can imagine was at a friends' daughter's wedding Sherry and I attended. It was beautiful, and the testimonies of the bride and groom caused us to rejoice with tears of joy! 11

Some of the fondest memories of unforgettable meals were at my grandma's house just down the street from us. A couple days before Thanksgiving, my mom would go down to help her mother prepare and all the children would get excited. Thanksgiving at Grandma's meant all our favorite dishes and desserts rarely shared during the year. After dinner, all the cousins would play games outside, and occasionally an adult or two would join us as we worked up an appetite for leftovers!

Sherry remembers Sunday dinners at her Momo and Papa's where 20-25 cousins, aunts and uncles gathered regularly and enjoyed fried chicken, roasts, potatoes, fresh garden vegetables in the summer and Momo's fruit cobblers still unmatched to this day!

At the Lambs Banquet no worries about anything a diabetic can't have. No worries about whether there is gluten or not. No worries about calories. No forbidden fruits. Everything everlasting beyond measure, no restrictions!
"No eye has seen, no ear has heard, and no mind can imagine what God has prepared for those who love Him" 1 Corinthians 2:9

......Centered Prayer.......

Father, I get excited imaging what a heavenly meal is going to be like. What an incredible day that will be when we sit with the Church to have the Lamb's Banquet with You. The joy will be overwhelming, the celebration indescribable. Praise will spring from our lips and lift to the rafters the glory and honor You deserve.

But until that day gets here, I commit to practice praising Your holy name. I will not wait until that day to sing of Your wonderful grace and mercy that You have showered over my life. I will honor You now with my walk of faith, with my treasurers however meager they may be, and with my whole life. I commit to be ready for the moment the bridegroom comes.

Thank You Father that I have the witness of Your Spirit to be part of Your family. What a day! What a day that will be!

11. Ministry Illustration, Oyer, Sherry [ret.], *Anna Banister Wedding,* Grand Rapids, Mi.

BANQUET REFLECTIONS

WHAT IS IT ABOUT THE LAMB'S PROMISED BANQUET THAT EXCITE ME?

COULD THAT EXCITEMENT BECOME SOMEHOW INTEGRATED INTO MY MEAL, OR TABLE CONVERSATION?

MY NOTES

RESOURCES
Taste and See ... Margaret Feinberg
Table Talk Magazine
Meeting Jesus at the Table ... Cynthia Campbell and Christine Fohr/Kevin Bacon
The Table Ministry of Jesus in Gospel of Luke ... Emma Rooker
The Three Tables ... R. David Jones
The Three Tables of Jesus ... James Hill
What is on the Menu at God's Table ... Jennifer Rothschild
The Dinner Table as a Place of Connectedness, Brokenness and
   Blessing.... Barry D. Jones
Table Host ... Mary Rearick Paul
Jesus Dinner Talk ... Verlon's Blog
Jesus Is Coming: Prepare the Table ... life: beautiful.
Setting a Beautiful Table: Hospitality at Lord's Supper ...
   Holiness Today, Nov/Dec. 2017
Jesus at the Table ... Brian Dennert
A Meal with Jesus: Discovering Grace, Community and Mission
Around the Table ... Tim Chester
Dinning with Jesus ... Kate Jackson
Meeting Jesus at the Dinner Table ... Manoj Raithatha
Simply Eat ... Evangelical Alliance

***At the Table Discussion Questions ... Taylor Walling

The Lord's Supper and the Great Banquet ... Dr. Ralph F. Wilson

The Easter Code: Day 22 [pg.48] ... O.J. Hawkins

Meals with Jesus ... Ed Drew

Come to the Table: A Celebration of Family Life ... Doris Christopher

Sunday Dinner ... Lora Lee Parrott

Dinner With The President ... Alex Pru'Homme, *Afred A. Knopf publisher*

Dinner with Ruth ... Nina Totenberg

Thank You

Every book, like every dinner, consists of different ingredients [in this case individuals] who have in some part contributed to bringing about a finished product. This chapter was exciting, yet a challenging one. I am delighted to acknowledge each deserving person, yet the nagging fear that I am forgetting someone shadowed every sentence. In this Thankyou there is no specific order, for regardless of the volume of thought and work contributed by each person a measure of true gratefulness is deserved.

The first individual to read this manuscript and give helpful insights is my friend Debbie Hausler. It was her encouragement for me to take the road to eventual publication, thanks Deb. The Individuals who work in the Traverse City Library Computer Lab who guided me through each manuscript copy were so kind and helpful. Then Heather Cartwright, Guy Wood, and Pastor Jack Harnish, read the manuscript and gave me corrective suggestions, and meaningful reviews. Elaine Wood also read the manuscript and gave editing tips. Enough thanks can't be given Jane Cavender, my main editor, and fellow devotional author herself, who coached and prodded me through numerous rewrites and brought the manuscript to publication. So many of those who contributed are authors themselves and benefiting from their experience was a blessing! Another amazing blessing was having Pastor Jon Carnes writing a prayer for every chapter, among the numerous books he has written is one titled Prayer & Fasting. Jon is the pastor at Pensacola Florida First Nazarene Church. There are individuals upon whom God has bestowed the gift of "the prayer language" and Pastor Jon is one of those. Translating his prayers to the Father must be a cake walk for the Spirit. During one of our dinners, we were hosting Rich and Carole Halmekangas, and I mentioned how the book "Dinner with the President" had influenced my manuscript and how it was with sadness I must return it to the library. About a week later a copy of that book arrived in the mail, a gift from Carole and Rich, I am on my fourth reading of it!

One of my richest blessings has been my wife Sherry, she read the manuscript numerous times and spent hours correcting, helped me title this book and reminded me of numerous dinners in our ministry that benefited from Jesus' example.

I am forever indebted to the Holy Spirit for instructive interruptions and inspiring moments.

I am also grateful for your taking the time to read this book and am excited to hear what your thoughts might be.

Email me at tsoyer2003@Yahoo.com.

Again, THANKYOU!